LETTERS TO YOUNG BLACK MEN

OTHER BOOKS
by
Daniel Whyte III

- *MO' LETTERS TO YOUNG BLACK MEN*

- *LETTERS TO YOUNG BLACK WOMEN*

- *WHEN BLACK PREACHERS PREACH Volume I*, Editor

- *WHEN BLACK PREACHERS PREACH Volume II*, Editor

- *WHEN BLACK PREACHERS PREACH Volume III*, Editor

- 7 THINGS YOUNG BLACK MEN DO TO MESS UP
  THEIR LIVES

- 7 THINGS YOUNG BLACK WOMEN DO TO MESS UP
  THEIR LIVES

- *MONEY UNDER THE CAR SEAT (AND OTHER
  THINGS TO THANK GOD FOR)*

- *GOD HAS SMILED ON ME: A TRIBUTE TO A BLACK
  FATHER WHO STAYED*

- *JUST JESUS: THE GREATEST THINGS EVER SAID
  ABOUT THE GREATEST MAN WHO EVER LIVED*,
  Editor

LETTERS TO YOUNG BLACK MEN

ADVICE AND ENCOURAGEMENT FOR A DIFFICULT JOURNEY

by
DANIEL WHYTE III

LETTERS TO YOUNG BLACK MEN

New, Revised Cover Design by Mr. Bill Hopper of Hopper Graphics of Texas.

Original Cover Design by Daniella Whyte and Daniel D. P. Whyte IV of WHYTEHOUSE DESIGNS, LTD.

The Bible quotations in this volume are from the King James Version of the Bible.

The name TORCH LEGACY PUBLICATIONS and its logo are registered as a trademark in the U.S. patent office.

ISBN 0-9763487-9-9

Printed in the USA.

WHAT PEOPLE ARE SAYING ABOUT
LETTERS TO YOUNG BLACK MEN
FROM ACROSS THE NATION

• "Without a doubt, this book will help young black men as they travel on life's journey. It is understandable and makes easy reading as it is written in simple everyday language. The book provides significant information, advice and encouragement to young black men that will help them to improve in all areas of their lives...This book is great reading and should be read by all young black men. I am confident that any reader will glean gems from this book."   **—Major Carl Bennett**, Tallahassee Sheriff's Department, Baptist Minister & Florida A & M Graduate, Tallahassee FL

• "Daniel Whyte's book is an eloquent, heart-felt plea for a more constructive and spiritual approach to one of America's most painful problems: the tragic waste of so many lives of our young black men."
          —Michael Medved, Nationally Syndicated Talk Show Host

• "It's a very valuable book to recommend to young men to read. I think it has a lot of potential and could have a good impact."
          —Pastor Dwight McKissic
          Senior Pastor, *Cornerstone Baptist Church,* Arlington, Texas
• "*Letters To Young Black Men* is a great book. I'm buying 40 for my church bookstore today."   **—Rev. Glendy Hamilton**, Pastor
          Harvest Baptist Church, Orlando, FL
• "This is a much needed book for our community. I think that this book is the capstone of Daniel Whyte's ministry. Every young black man in America should read this book."   **—Rev. Sammie Madison**, President
          Intelligent Faith Ministries, Atlanta, GA
• "Daniel Whyte III has knocked a home run with this book, *Letters To Young Black Men*. It is a timely book. It is powerful. And it is a life-changing book. We need to get it into the hands of every young black man."
          —Pastor Valice Cuthbertson, Charlotte, NC
• "*Letters To Young Black Men* is a great book. I highly recommend it."
          —Rev. Andrew Hamilton, Pastor
          Berean Baptist Church, Thomasville, GA

• First and foremost, I would like to thank you for walking the journey that you are on. I was in Wal-Mart looking for a gift for a co-worker. While looking through the aisles, I came across your book, *Letters To Young Black Men*. I am an adamant reader, and I am trying to move my son in this direction. My son has been having some discipline and focus issues. I have been seeking out different possible mentor programs for him, but so far I have not come up with anything. Well, I saw your book and my son just came to mind. I began to read some of the letters and chapter titles and immediately made the purchase. I am going to give him the book as a Christmas gift to hopefully add to the interest of reading it. My son is 12 years old and very smart. I work with him all the time and make frequent visits to his school to try and stay on top of things; however, I want to ensure I am doing all I can to help my son succeed. Any information you can provide would be greatly appreciated! Thank you again, and God bless!

—Mrs. Z. Liddell

• I just finished reading your book, *"LETTERS TO YOUNG BLACK MEN"* and I am writing to commend you and thank you for writing it. I am making a list of folks that will be getting your book as a Christmas gift. And that includes my own two sons. Thank you for the manner/style that it was written in: personable, real, to the point, and with obvious love. I imagine that this writing style will easily be accepted from a male point of view. From a female point of view, it really touched my heart. I have a son who is currently in prison, 16 years, but will be coming home soon. Your book, along with a few others, i.e; the BIBLE, will give instruction and help to get him re-started in the right direction. Thank you again and God bless.

—Mrs. M. L. Hill

• This book is an inspirational work for the reader. It explores the three aspects of life that causes conflicts and problems in the life of young men: the spiritual, mental, and emotional aspects of life that for so long has gone unaddressed are delved into in detail. Although the book talks about young black men, this is a lesson for all young men.

—Mr. Douglas L. Spellman, *Texas Wesleyan University*

• I picked up this book in a gas station somewhere between North Carolina and Virginia. I have a 19-year old away at school. He was brought up in the church and, quite honestly, he likes going to church. We've never had problems getting him to participate in church activities. So I feel he has the religious roots to stand on. However, being away from home, I know he is being challenged in his church attendance. More importantly, I want him to "know the Lord," not just attend church. Flipping through the book at the store aroused enough of my interest to purchase it. I read it first before giving it to my son and was even more impressed. That is when I ordered 10 more to give to my husband, pastor, nephews, cousins, and brother-in-law, who is being deployed to Kuwait. I gave the book to my son the week before his Spring Break and told him I expected him to read it once, twice or as many times as necessary over Spring Break to get the message. He truly surprised me and called to tell me he was almost done with it the week I gave it to him. My note inside the book said to him to pass it on to a friend if it benefitted him. He said he had highlighted so much of the book, he wanted to keep his and could I send him 2 more to give to his room mates. (Yesterday he wanted 2 more for others who saw him reading it.) I have not heard from my nephews that I gave it to. They may need a little more encouragement to read it, but that's why I gave it to them. They truly need "encouragement for a difficult journey". Every Black young man that I know I want to share this with them and their parents. Some co-workers asked for some too. I teach Sunday School, ages 8-11, and I will use the section entitled, "Things I wished someone had told me at age 12" with my class.

—Mrs. B. Denson

This book is lovingly dedicated to my

Dad,

Daniel White Jr.,

My brothers:

Anthony Martin & Mark A.White,

My sons:

Daniel IV, Duran and Danyel,

My Daughters:

Daniella, Danita, Danielle, Danae`, Daniqua and
Danyelle,

who I hope will find good young black men, if that is

God's will for their lives,

And to

All young black men across America and

around the world.

LETTERS TO YOUNG BLACK MEN

CONTENTS

ACKNOWLEDGMENTS

Above all, I wish to thank God for putting within my heart a desire to do a work such as this. I also wish to thank my wife, Meriqua, who said, "Daddy, you can do it," and then helped me to do it by typing the first manuscript. My secretary, Tracie Thomas deserves special gratitude for her wise input, encouragement and faithful, hard work. Additionally, let me thank my two assistants in the work of the ministry, Louis Allen and Patrick Foster, both of whom not only served as inspiration to write this book, but also gave me honest and encouraging feedback. I especially, want to thank my daughter, Daniella, and my son, Daniel IV, for typesetting and proofreading the second manuscript and for designing the cover. And I also want to thank all of my other children for inspiring me to write this book and for being obedient, quiet and patient as I worked.

Additionally, for this second revised and expanded edition of *Letters to Young Black Men*, I must especially thank Dr. Melissa Russell, adjunct professor of Languages & Literature at Texas Wesleyan University for editing the manuscript; Mr. Bill Hopper of Hopper Graphics of Texas for redesigning the cover; Mr. Ron T. Smith, Mrs. Edna Byrd, and the staff of Bookworld Companies — our bookstore and library distributor; and Mr. Simon Schrock, Eldon Schrock, and Choice Books Distributors, for helping to make *Letters to Young Black Men* a national bestseller. I would also like to thank Mr. Pete Hoelzl, Mrs. Stella Cazares, and their fine staff for doing a great job in printing the book.

LETTERS TO YOUNG BLACK MEN

INTRODUCTION

It appears that many people are concerned about the worsening conditions in the black community of America. And let's just be honest: we are in a bad way, generally speaking. I say, "generally speaking," because there are some blacks who are not doing badly at all. But the black community, in general, is not doing that well. You don't believe that? Just read the newspaper: we're killing one another, robbing our parents and grandparents, raping our women, selling death to the dying, going to jail wholesale, murdering our babies, not taking care of our responsibilities, and wiping out our future.

Why are we sinking in the sea of murder, drugs and mayhem? How can things be turned around? I believe that the problem lies largely with the black man, and I also believe that the solution lies with the black man. I am convinced that the key to turning black America around is to turn black men around. For any group of people to rise, their men must rise. And after they have risen, they must stay standing no matter what, and take their God-given position as the leaders of their families, churches, communities or what have you. These letters aim to help with that rising and standing.

These letters have been written in the midst of a very hectic schedule of traveling, editing an international publication, and working on several other publishing projects. These letters have also been written in the midst of being a black man, and a black husband and father, with all of the great and awful experiences that go with such an existence. I said that to say this: As I write these letters, I am not in some ivory tower somewhere philosophizing about life as a young black man. Rather, I am right in the middle of life as a young black man.

In short, these letters come from a sincere heart of a black man to the hearts of young black men.

Dear Y.B.M. (Please note that Y.B.M. will stand for "Young Black Man" throughout the book): I believe that this is a book that can absolutely revolutionize your life if you will let it.

See this book as a sign-post on the road of life, pointing you in the right direction. Read it, read it again, and then pass it on to another young black man struggling to find his way in this sometimes confusing and hostile world.

Daniel Whyte **III**
Tuskegee University Campus
Tuskegee, Alabama

LETTERS TO YOUNG BLACK MEN IS CHANGING HEARTS & LIVES

"I am a twenty-year-old African-American male, and I must say that this book has turned my life around for the good. I would recommend this book to anyone, especially YBM (young black men) such as myself. This book has inspired me to start a YBM's ministry at my church where once a week we, the YBM of this generation, will get together, read the book, then discuss it. I think this will really help the YBM in the church and even the ones who are not in the church. I hope I can make it happen. Thanks for the inspiration."

—Delvon Glover

NEVER
UNDERESTIMATE A
YOUNG BLACK
MAN

—Daniel Whyte III

NEVER GIVE UP ON A YOUNG BLACK MAN — BECAUSE YOU NEVER KNOW...

—Daniel Whyte III

TO OLDER BLACK MEN:
NEVER AGAIN FORGET
ABOUT, CAST ASIDE,
NEGLECT OR MISTREAT A
YOUNG BLACK MAN, FOR
THEY WILL GROW OLDER
AND REMEMBER YOU

—Daniel Whyte III

IF YOU CONSIDER YOURSELF YOUNG, SIR, THEN YOU ARE YOUNG

—Daniel Whyte III

ON YOUR
LIFE – SPIRITUAL

THE MAIN THING

Letter One

Dear Y.B.M.:

I am writing this letter from Hamden, Connecticut. I trust that you are doing well in these days.

Recently, I was speaking at a church in Orlando, Florida, and I saw a sign on the front of the pulpit that read:

> **The Main Thing**
> **Is To Keep**
> **The Main Thing**
> **The Main Thing.**

In this, my first letter to you, I would like to speak to you about the most important aspect of your life — your Spiritual Life: the Main Thing. Now, you may not now think that your spiritual life is the most important part of your life, but trust me, it is. The longer you live on planet earth, the more you realize that life is more about the inner man than the outer man; for you see, you are not a body with a spirit. Rather, you are a spirit with a body. If your physical body would fall away, you would still exist.

Jesus said: ***"Man shall not live by bread alone, but by every word that proceedeth out of the mouth of God."***
—Matthew 4:4

I realize that talking about things spiritual is not popular these days, and it may not be what you wish to talk about at this time. I recall, when I was a child and got sick with what they called the "whooping cough" or some type of flu or cold, my dear grandmother Beaman and/or my great-grandmother Breedlove would give me something that I didn't like — but needed. It was called "Castor Oil". Dear Y.B.M., you may not like all that I am talking with you about, or you may not be interested in what I am talking with you about, but being that I have gone the way that you are going, I can say firmly and lovingly that you need it! Before we talk about things that may seemingly be of more interest to you, we must put the horse before the cart. We must put first things first.

Your spiritual life, your relationship with God, should be your number one priority in this life. No, it is not your health, your wealth, or even your education. It is God and God alone! There was a time that we as a race of people put more of an emphasis on the spiritual life than we do now. Today, however, we place more of an emphasis on the body, material things and money. And we wonder why we have the murder, mayhem and madness in our community!

Young man, you can be a part of turning things around for your people. But you must put God first and make your spiritual life priority number one.

Jesus also said: *"For what shall it profit a man, if he shall gain the whole world, and lose his own soul?"*

—Mark 8:36

Yours For Putting God First,

Daniel Whyte III

P.S.: Throughout this book, instead of having P.S.'s, I will use P.T.'s for "Power Thoughts."

P.T. (Power Thoughts):

- "One with God is a majority."
  —Billy Graham

- "America has abandoned the strong woman of spirituality and is shacking up with the harlot of materialism."
  —Joseph Lowery

- "He who provides for this life, but takes no care for eternity, is wise for a moment, but a fool forever."
  —Tillotson

- "The greatest riches of our community are not material but moral."
  —David N. Dinkins

- "It is our duty to conserve our physical powers, our intellectual endowments, our spiritual ideals."
  —W. E. B. Du Bois

GET TO KNOW YOUR CREATOR

Letter Two

Dear Y.B.M.:

I trust that you are doing well today. I am doing fine.

If you have not done so already, may I strongly encourage you to get to know your God? Dear friend, you will not have a happy, fulfilling, successful life without God as your center. It simply will not happen.

Now when I say get to know God, I am not talking about joining a church, getting baptized, doing good works, or becoming more active in church. I am talking about getting to know God personally for yourself. Here is what I mean:

First of all**, understand that you are a sinner like the rest of us.** Yes, believe it or not, each of us born into this world has sinned. Each one of us has broken the laws of God. The Bible states plainly:

"For all have sinned and come short of the glory of God."
—Romans 3:23

Second, **God wants us to understand that because of our sin, there is a great punishment and that punishment is death — both spiritual death and physical death**. You see, because of sin, we not only die physically, but also because of sin we die spiritually. This spiritual death is actually eternal separation from God in a place called Hell. Notice what God's Word says about this death:

"For the wages of sin is death…" —Romans 6:23

"But the fearful, and unbelieving, and the abominable, and murderers and whoremongers, and sorcerers, and idolaters, and all liars, shall have their part in the lake which burneth with fire and brimstone: which is the second death."
—Revelation 21:8

Third, **after realizing our sad and condemned condition, God wants us to understand that He loves us more than we love ourselves**. He loves us so much that He sent His only Son, Jesus Christ, to live, suffer, shed His blood and die on Calvary's cross for your sin and mine. After Jesus' earth-shaking death that day, He was buried and three days later He arose again by the power of God. You remember this verse, don't you? You probably learned it in Sunday School when you were a child:

"For God so loved the world, that He gave His only begotten Son, that whosoever believeth in him should not perish, but have everlasting life."
—John 3:16

In order to really know God, you must go through His only begotten Son, Jesus Christ. Notice what Jesus Christ said Himself:

"I am the way, the truth, and the life: no man cometh unto the Father, but by me."
—John 14:6

Jesus Christ is the only way to God. Jesus Christ is the only way to joy, peace and to eternal life. Here is how to accept Him into your heart according to the scriptures:

"That if thou shalt confess with thy mouth the Lord Jesus, and shalt believe in thine heart that God hath raised him from the dead, thou shalt be saved." —Romans 10:9

"For whosoever shall call upon the name of the Lord shall be saved." —Romans 10:13

Dear friend of mine, if you want to know God, the source of all love, joy, peace, real happiness and true success, believe in your heart that Jesus Christ died, was buried and rose again for you, and ask Him to come into your heart and save you. And He will. You have God's Word on it.

In His Amazing Grace,

Daniel Whyte III

P.T.:

■ "Our salvation comes to us so easily because it cost God so much."
—Oswald Chambers

■ "So, Pastor McKinney, you must think you are saved because you are a good fellow." "No, I am not a good fellow. I just have a good Saviour."
—Charles McKinney

■ "No man is ever the same after God has laid His hand upon him."
—A. W. Tozer

■ "Only through an inner spiritual transformation do we gain the strength to fight victoriously the evils of the world in a humble and loving spirit."
—Dr. Martin Luther King, Jr.

■ "Death is not the end for someone who has faith in Jesus Christ."
—Bishop Desmond Tutu

■ "I am ready to die, not because I have lived as well as I should have; I am ready to die because Jesus lived and died so well for me."
—Daniel Whyte III

HOW TO OBTAIN THE BLESSINGS OF GOD

Letter Three

Dear Y.B.M.:

At this writing, I am sitting in my vehicle in front of a United Parcel Service office in Hamden, Connecticut, waiting for them to open so that I can pick up an important package.

By the way, so that you will know, due to the nature of my work, I travel a lot, so I will be writing these letters from all over the United States. I was born in Brooklyn, New York, mostly raised in New Bern, North Carolina, and at this writing I reside in Atlanta, Georgia.

I trust that you have come to know your Creator, God, by believing in His Son, Jesus Christ as your Saviour. That is, indeed, the most important thing that you will ever do in your life. Congratulations, if you have made that all important decision. If perhaps you have not done so, please do not procrastinate, for tomorrow, as they say, is not promised you.

Now, in this letter, I would like to share with you how it is that you can obtain the coveted blessings of God in this life. Those who are genuinely happy and successful in this life are those who have been blessed by God. You may ask, "well, what is a blessing, anyway?" I've heard older folks in my family use the term often, and I myself used to wonder, "What is a blessing?" Well, according to *Webster's Third New International Dictionary*, it means:

> To make happy: give good fortune or satisfaction to; confer prosperity upon...

According to the *Nelson Bible Dictionary* **blessed** means:

> God blesses people by granting prosperity or
> well-being in the form of both physical and
> spiritual grace.

And according to the *New Westminister Dictionary of the Bible*,
blessed or **blessing** means:

> To bestow divine favor and confer divine benefits.
> Favors, advantages, conferred by God, and
> bringing pleasure or happiness in their lives.

From these definitions, friend, we see that blessings from God are
very important in this life if we are to be truly happy and prosperous.
How can we as young black men obtain these needed blessings for
our lives?

First of all, **we must have the right attitude toward our parents**.
Regardless of your home situation, those who are considered your
parents and/or guardians, are deserving of your love, respect and
honor. Even after you are grown and out on your own, you ought to
respect and honor your parents even though you may disagree with
them and travel your own path. And no matter what your age, if
you are still under your parents' roof and authority, you ought to
obey them as the Bible states:

*"Children, obey your parents in the Lord: For this is right.
Honour thy father and mother, which is the first
commandment with promise; that it may be well with thee,
and thou mayest live long on the earth."*

—Ephesians 6: 1-3

Second, **in order to receive God's blessings upon your life, you must choose to live a life that is obedient to God's Word**. This does not mean that you will be perfect, and it does not mean you will never sin again. It means that you will strive, with God's help, to be obedient to Him and when you sin, or make a mistake, you will quickly confess your sin and forsake it. Probably the most important lesson that I have learned since I have become a Christian is that GOD BLESSES OBEDIENCE, AND HE DOES NOT BLESS DISOBEDIENCE. HE NEVER HAS AND HE NEVER WILL! I have learned this from the Holy Scriptures as well as from painful personal experience. Hear God's Word on it:

"Behold, I set before you this day a blessing and a curse; A blessing, if ye obey the commandments of the Lord your God, which I command you this day. And a curse, if ye will not obey the commandments of the Lord your God, but turn aside out of the way which I command you this day, to go after other gods, which ye have not known."

—Deuteronomy 11: 26-28

Third, **we must spend quality time in prayer if we want God's blessings upon our lives**. Notice what Jesus Christ said on this matter of prayer:

"Ask, and it shall be given you; seek, and ye shall find; knock, and it shall be opened unto you: For everyone that asketh receiveth, and He that seeketh findeth, and to him that knocketh it shall be opened. Or what man is there of you, whom if his son ask bread, will he give him a stone? Or if he ask a fish, will he give him a serpent? If ye then, being evil, know how to give good gifts unto your children, how much more shall your Father which is in heaven give good things to them that ask him?"
—Matthew 7: 7-11

Prayer is where you will find great power for life and great blessings from God. May I kindly encourage you to pray often? God will hear and answer your prayers and bless you.

Fourth, **if we want to be blessed, we must have faith in God.**

As you go through this life as a young black man, it will behoove you to have strong faith in God. No matter what you face in this life, or what you may go through, always remember that God has all power in His hands and He is able to work it out. You may ask, "well, how can I build up and strengthen my faith?" Notice these words from the Bible:

"So then faith cometh by hearing, and hearing by the word of God."

—Romans 10:17

For a stronger faith, for a more dynamic faith, spend some quality time each day reading the Bible.

Last, **but certainly not least, let me encourage you to get into the habit of giving**. God blesses giving. Give to God through your local church. Give to others in need as you are led. Now, we do not give to get, but the simple fact is that when you give to God and others, God gives back to you. Like the old preachers used to say and still say, "You can't beat God giving, no matter how hard you try." And that is so true. Listen to what Jesus says about giving:

"Give, and it shall be given unto you; good measure, pressed down, and shaken together, and running over, shall men give into your bosom. For with the same measure that ye mete withal it shall be measured to you again."

—Luke 6:38

40

It is a fact: the more you give, the more God gives to you in so many different ways.

Friend, I apologize for this rather "long-winded" letter this time around. I just want you to obtain the blessings of God on your life.

Blessed,

Daniel

P.T.:

■ "The way each day will look to you all starts with who you're looking to."
—Selected

■ "I will lift up mine eyes unto the hills, from whence cometh my help. My help cometh from the Lord, which made heaven and earth."
—Psalm 121: 1

■ "Every work of God can be traced to some kneeling form."
—D. L. Moody

YOUR ROAD MAP TO REAL AND LASTING SUCCESS

Letter Four

Dear Y.B.M.:

I trust that you have been doing well since my last letter. Today, I am writing this letter from the law library at Yale University in New Haven, Connecticut. By the way, I just had a long and interesting conversation with a young black man who is a law student here.

In this letter, I want to expand on something that I barely touched on in a previous letter: i.e., the importance of the Bible in your life. Frankly, if you desire to be truly successful in life, you will need to read, meditate upon, and obey the Bible. In doing so, God promises good success. Notice what God says in Joshua 1:8:

"This book of the law shall not depart out of thy mouth; but thou shalt meditate therein day and night, that thou mayest observe to do according to all that is written therein: for then thou shalt make thy way prosperous, and then thou shalt have good success."

Do you want genuine, lasting success? If you do, you will have to make God's Word a vital part of your daily life. Your doing so, will guarantee success.

How should you read the Bible? Well, read it as often as God leads you to. And here are some additional, well-tested suggestions:

1. **Pray, Then Read**. Praying and reading the Bible go hand in hand. A good practice is to pray and ask God to open your spiritual

eyes before you read so that He can help you understand what you are reading. For you see, the Bible is a spiritual book, and it will take the Holy Spirit of God to teach it to you.

2. **Read And Retain** so that you can meditate upon what you read. To meditate means to think upon, and you cannot think upon something that you can't remember. Please don't be like the man who looked in the mirror and one second after looking in the mirror, forgot how he looked.

3. **Read And Obey**. You and I will never be perfect this side of Heaven. But God wants us to strive to obey His Word. And, of course, this is for our own good. Don't just be a hearer of God's Word, but a doer as well.

If, perhaps, you are just starting out in reading the Bible, may I suggest reading a chapter in the New Testament in the morning before leaving home and then reading a chapter in the Old Testament before going to sleep at night. It is good to have the Bible on your subconscious mind throughout the night. Later, as you grow, you may want to increase that to two chapters in the morning and two at night.

There are many benefits of reading and meditating upon the Bible. Here are just a few:

> 1. It will make you wise.
> 2. It will give you direction in life.
> 3. It will strengthen, fortify and stabilize you.
> 4. It will help you to help others.
> 5. It will make you genuinely successful.

As I wrap up this letter, let me leave you with what some successful people have said about the Bible and its greatness over the decades:

I believe the Bible is the best gift God has ever given to man. All the good from the Saviour of the world is communicated to us through this book.

—Abraham Lincoln

It is impossible to rightly govern the world without God and the Bible.

—George Washington

The Bible is no mere book, but a living creature, with a power that conquers all that oppose it.

—Napoleon

The Bible contains the mind of God, the state of man, the way of salvation, the doom of sinners, and the happiness of believers. Its doctrines are holy, its precepts are binding, its histories are true, and its decisions are immutable. Read it to be wise, believe it to be safe, and practice it to be holy. It contains light to direct you, food to support you, and comfort to cheer you.

It is the traveler's map, the pilgrim's staff, the pilot's compass, the soldier's sword, and the Christian's charter. Here Paradise is restored, Heaven opened, and the gates of hell disclosed.

Christ is the grand subject, our good the design, and the glory of God its end.

It should fill the memory, rule the heart, and guide the feet. Read it slowly, frequently, and prayerfully. It is a mine of wealth, a paradise of glory, and a river of pleasure. It is given you in life, will be opened at the judgement, and be remembered forever. It involves the highest responsibility, will reward the greatest labor, and will condemn all who trifle with its sacred contents.

—The Gideons

Read, study and love your Bible. It is the road map to true success.

With the Bible in my hand,

Daniel Whyte III

P.T.:

■ "The Bible humbles or hardens the human heart. We have to do something about its message, for we cannot leave it alone. We may think we have done nothing about it, but it will do something to us."

—Vance Havner

■ "Thy word is a lamp unto my feet, and a light unto my path."

—Psalm 119:105

46

■ "The key to my understanding of the Bible is...personal relationship to Jesus Christ."
—Oswald Chambers

■ "Nobody ever outgrows Scripture; the book widens and deepens with our years."
—C. H. Spurgeon

TAP INTO UNLIMITED POWER

Letter Five

Dear Y.B.M.:

I trust that you and yours are doing well.

You may be wondering, once again, why I am writing to you so much on spiritual matters. Well, the reason is, as I said to you earlier, the spiritual aspect of your life is the most important part of your life. It is the very center of your existence. If you get this part of your life in order, everything else will fall into place. Jesus Christ said:

"But seek ye first the kingdom of God, and his righteousness; and all these things shall be added unto you."
—Matthew 6: 33

In this letter, I want to speak to you specifically about the all important matter of prayer. There is great power through prayer to God. And there are great benefits from God in prayer. You will find as you trail through life that you will need God, and prayer invites God to work in, through, and for your life. Notice what God says through His prophet Jeremiah as to what He (God) will do if you pray:

"Thus saith the Lord the maker thereof, the Lord that formed it, to establish it; the LORD is his name; Call unto me, and I will answer thee, and shew thee great and mighty things, which thou knowest not."
—Jeremiah 33: 2-3

49

Even though Jesus Christ is God, He still spent quality time in prayer while He was upon planet earth. You may recall that one time He got up a "great while before day" (Mark 1:35) and prayed. On another occasion, He taught His disciples how to pray; and then in the Garden of Gethsemane before His crucifixion, He prayed earnestly and fervently. And then at another time, *"He spake a parable unto them to this end that men ought always to pray and not to faint."* (Luke 18:1)

As you can see, prayer is highly esteemed in the sight of God. I lovingly urge you to make prayer an integral part of your daily life. Here are some of the great benefits that I have found through prayer:

1. The Almighty God has liberty to work in your life.

2. Through prayer, we invite God to lead us and guide us through the labyrinth of life.

3. Through prayer, we can receive the very wisdom of God.

4. Through prayer, we can gain the power of the Holy Spirit to do that which is right.

5. Through prayer, we can gain peace of heart and mind no matter what we are going through.

6. Through prayer, we can gain the boldness, courage and confidence to help others.

7. Through prayer, we can find favor in the sight of God and man.

8. Through prayer, we can obtain financial, material and physical blessings.

These are just some of the blessings that I have received through prayer unto God. I can say not only in theory, but by experience, that "Prayer changes things." Prayer has changed my life and it can change yours as well.

As I close this letter, dear friend, I would like to leave you with some suggestions on how to pray and when to pray. First, the best and only pattern to follow that our Lord gave to us is what is commonly called "The Lord's Prayer," which is found in Matthew 6: 9-13:

"After this manner therefore pray ye: Our Father which art in heaven, Hallowed be thy name. Thy kingdom come. Thy will be done in earth, as it is in heaven. Give us this day our daily bread. And forgive us our debts, as we forgive our debtors. And lead us not into temptation, but deliver us from evil: For thine is the kingdom, and the power, and the glory, for ever. Amen."

Now you do not have to pray this same prayer, but you can use it as a guide in your own prayer life. According to Jesus' pattern of prayer, you should:

1. Praise God first.
2. Put His will before yours.
3. Ask for your daily provisions.
4. Ask for forgiveness of sin.
5. Ask God to keep you from evil.
6. Give God the glory.

Lay everything on your heart and mind before God and enjoy His peace.

As far as when to pray, pray as God leads you, as I mentioned to you in a previous letter. But it is also good to follow the example of David and Daniel of old and pray at appointed times. In other words, schedule your time so that you include special quality periods in your day for nothing else but for prayer unto God. It is good to keep regular times to pray as well as to pray in between those times as God's Holy Spirit prompts you.

Keep praying, for prayer is truly where the power is.

Prayerfully Yours,

Daniel

P.T.:

■ "Prayer succeeds when all else fails."

—E. M. Bounds

■ "We must focus on prayer as the main thrust to accomplish God's will and purpose on earth. The forces against us have never been greater and this is the only way we can release God's power to become victorious."

—John Maxwell

■ "Man is a being of spirit."

—Dr. Martin Luther King, Jr

■ "Prayer does not equip us for greater works — prayer is the greater work."

—Oswald Chambers

■ "I learned as never before that persistent calling upon the Lord breaks through every stronghold of the devil, for nothing is impossible with God. For Christians in these troubled times, there is simply no other way."

—Jim Cymbala

■ "Prayer is never the least we can do."

—A. W. Tozer

THE ENCOURAGEMENT PLACE

Letter Six

Dear Y.B.M.:

Down through the years in this country, we as a people have been known to be closely connected to the church.

My grandparents and parents are church-going people. They always have been. I am thankful that my elders made sure that I went to church regularly while I was growing up. I must say that I really did not learn much from church during those years. But I am thankful for the experience because it helped to place within me a hunger and desire for the true and living God.

When I became a teenager, I rebelled against going to church. During that time, I did not feel that it had any place in my life. However, when I left home upon graduation from high school, God and the church had a strong pull on me, even though I was a prodigal son. After some time out on my own, I finally came to know the true and living God through Jesus Christ. I believe this grand experience is due partly to my praying grandparents and parents and their dogged resolution to keep their offspring in church. I said all of that to say this: **Stay close to the church**.

If you have trusted Jesus Christ as your personal Saviour, you ought to be involved in a good church. Why?

1. **Because God wants you to be.**

"Not forsaking the assembling of ourselves together, as the manner of some is, but exhorting one another: and so much

the more, as ye see the day approaching."

—Hebrews 10:25

2. Because going to church regularly will strengthen and build up your faith through the preaching and teaching of God's Word.

"So then faith cometh by hearing, and hearing by the Word of God."

—Romans 10:17

3. **Because it gives you the opportunity and priviledge to worship and serve God through hearing His word, public prayers, singing, teaching, ushering, and helping others, etc**.

4. **It also gives you the joy and priviledge to exhort others and to be exhorted yourself**. The word "exhort" means to urge and encourage to keep going on strong for God. You will find, in this life, that you will need that encouragement often.

When I discuss attending church, I am not talking about going to just any church. Everything that has church on its sign is not necessarily a church. But I don't have to tell you that. When you look for a church, look for these things:

A. Is the pastor a born-again Christian himself? (I know that may sound strange, but you'll be surprised.)

B. Are the pastor and teachers preaching and teaching from the Bible as it is written?

C. Does the pastor and church believe and stand on the essentials of the Christian faith? (1) The Virgin Birth of Jesus Christ (2)

56

The Deity of Jesus Christ (that Jesus Christ is God) (3) The Resurrection of Jesus Christ (4) The Second Coming of Jesus Christ (5) and the Infallibility of the Scriptures (that the Bible is truly God's Word without error).

D. Is it a church that carries out the "Great Commission"? (i.e., tells others about Jesus Christ):

"Go ye therefore, and teach all nations, baptizing them in the name of the Father, and of the Son, and of the Holy Ghost: Teaching them to observe all things whatsoever I have commanded you: and, lo, I am with you alway, even unto the end of the world. Amen."

—Matthew 28:19-20

E. No church will be perfect. (And, as they say, if you find the perfect church, once you join it, it won't be perfect anymore.) No, there is no such thing as a perfect church. But the leaders and people ought to strive by the grace of God to live according to the Bible.

These are some of the main things to look for in a church before joining it.

Now once you find a good church, go regularly and go with the following:

• Go with the right attitude. Expect God to bless you and meet your needs.

• Go with a humble spirit. Don't go to be seen.

• Go with a praying heart. Ask God to bless the meeting.

• Go to worship God and give Him the glory.

Clear your schedule for God's house and God will richly bless you through His church that He has established for your good.

Going to Church,

Daniel

P.T.: Bro. Blaine Bartel - National Director of "Oneighty" and author of *The Little Black Book* series says the following:

FOUR REASONS WHY YOU NEED A GOOD PASTOR

1. A good pastor will protect you from wolves. A good pastor has a shepherd's heart and will warn you, helping you steer clear of people and situations that could destroy you.
2. A good pastor will feed you. Without spiritual food you will slowly suffer spiritual malnutrition, losing the strength you need to be victorious every day in life. Each time you sit under God's Word you are feeding on spiritual nutrients.
3. A good pastor will inspire you. God will use your pastor to open your heart and mind to the dreams and vision God has for you.
4. A good pastor will correct you. (2 Tim. 4:2) Good pastors are not afraid to bring rebuke and correction that will keep us from getting in a ditch. God will supernaturally lead them to say things that are exactly what you need to hear each week.

PULLING OTHERS OUT OF THE FIRE

Letter Seven

Dear Y.B.M.:

If you have applied what I have shared with you in the previous six letters, you are on the right track to a genuinely successful and fulfilling life. In this letter, I want to talk with you about "*pulling others out of the fire*."

Since my first letter to you, God has probably blessed you in some very special ways: you have become a Christian, you have direction in your life, you are communicating with God through prayer and through His Word, and you are seeing things in a different way now. I am sure, even in this short time, that you have realized the value and importance of having God as the center of your life.

Since God has blessed you so, dear friend, He wants you, in turn, to be a blessing to others. Jesus Christ once said to His disciples: *"Freely ye have received, freely give"* (Matthew 10:8). Look around you and see the devastation in many of our black communities. Many of our people are presently "in the fire," so to speak. Some are in the fire of living an absolutely purposeless life. Some are in the fire of drugs and alcohol. Many of our young black men are in the fire of jail and prison. Some of our people are suffering from the fire of the consequences of illicit sexual activities like babies having babies, AIDS and other venereal diseases. But, even sadder, is the fact that many of our people are headed to the fires of hell.

With the light and knowledge you have received already, you can be used of God to help pull our people out of the fire. How can you do that? First, you must understand that it will not be done through social programs alone; it will not be done through education alone; and it will not be done through the government alone. The main solution to the problems that we face in the black community is God Himself and the principles made plain in His Word. If we are to help turn our community around in a very real way, it will only be through the gospel of Jesus Christ and the correct teaching and application of His Word.

Before one can solve his own problems of drugs, alcoholism, illicit sexual behaviour, etc., he must deal with the root problem, and his root problem is the same problem faced by every other man: SIN. The only way that we can solve the sin problem is through Jesus Christ. And the way that we can help rescue our people from the fires of eternal punishment, as well as the fires caused by the sin of our lives, is by sharing with them what is called God's plan of salvation out of the Bible. Here is how:

First, **show them from God's Word that "We are all sinners**."

"For all have sinned and come short of the glory of God."
—Saint Paul, Romans 3:23

Second, **show them that there is a great punishment for sin: that is, eternal separation from God in a place called hell**.

"For the wages of sin is death…"
—Saint Paul, Romans 6:23

"And fear not them which kill the body but are not able to kill the soul: but rather fear him which is able to destroy both soul and body in hell."
—Jesus Christ, Matthew 10:28

Third, **show them that inspite of their sin, God still loves them and wants to save them.**

"For God so loved the world, that he gave his only begotten Son, that whosoever believeth in him should not perish, but have everlasting life."

—Jesus Christ, John 3:16

Last, **show them that all they have to do to be saved is trust in Jesus Christ.**

"That if thou shalt confess with thy mouth the Lord Jesus, and shalt believe in thine heart that God hath raised him from the dead, thou shalt be saved."

"For whosoever shall call upon the name of the Lord shall be saved."

—Saint Paul, Romans 10: 9 & 13

Of course, after a person trusts Jesus Christ for salvation, that is only the beginning. After that, he should join a good Bible preaching and teaching church, get baptized and be discipled. And with the plain teaching of the Bible by the pastor and you, and with the working of the Holy Spirit of God in the individual's life, many of the other fires that may be burning in the new convert's life will begin to be extinguished.

Pulling Folks Out Of The Fire,

Daniel

P.T.:

■ "A Christian must keep the faith, but not to himself."

—Jim Patrick

61

ON YOUR
LIFE – EDUCATIONAL

THE AWESOME VALUE OF READING

Letter Eight

Dear Y.B.M.:

This letter will be quite different from my previous letters in that I will not deal with the spiritual aspect of life, but rather the mental aspect of life.

First of all, may I kindly encourage you to spend as much time as you possibly can reading? At the writing of this letter, I am sitting in the Barnes & Noble bookstore in Hamden, Connecticut. Besides the library, a good bookstore is my next favorite place to be. If I am not careful, I can spend an entire day in a good bookstore. I go to libraries and bookstores often. When I go, there is always one thing that troubles me, however, and that is the conspicuous absence of young black men.

Why is it that many of us young black men do not read much? First, I believe that it is because many of us as young black boys were simply not turned on to reading as many of our white counterparts were. Rather, we were turned on to a heavy diet of television and sports. Another reason is because many of us had the wrong mentality and attitude about school while growing up. Instead of seeing it as a golden opportunity, we saw it as a place to skip, fight, run the girls, and as we got older, to party. Therefore, sadly, many of us missed out on gaining the importance and joy of reading. However, thankfully, it is never too late to start reading.

I am still sitting in the Barnes & Noble bookstore and every person walking through the door is a white male with the exception of one white female. Could it be that these people know something that we don't? (By the way, in case you're wondering, black people live all around this bookstore.)

You may ask: Well what is the big deal about reading? What are the benefits of reading, anyway? I am glad you asked. Consider with me some of the benefits of reading:

1. Through regular reading, you can become an "educated person" without following a rigid course of study.

2. Regular reading forces you to increase your vocabulary.

3. Through regular reading you can become a more interesting person to talk with.

4. Through regular reading, you are able to go places, mentally, that you may not be in a position to go physically.

5. Regular reading will help you become a better writer, speller and speaker.

6. Regular reading helps you to become a thinker.

7. Regular reading puts you head and shoulders above the crowd. As they say, "Readers are leaders."

To help get you started in a fulfilling life of reading, if you have not started already, here are some suggested areas that you can explore outside of the Book of books – the Bible:

A. Read a good grammar book through a couple of times. This will help you immensely in so many areas.

B. Read a pocket dictionary through, over a good space of time, of course. (A page a day is a good pace.)

C. Read a good short history of the world. This will help give you a broader perspective on what is happening today.

D. Read a good history of Africa. This will help you to understand where you came from.

E. Read a couple of good Black American History books. This will help you to understand who you are.

F. Read the classics written by both black and white authors. These books will strengthen your vocabulary as well as put you in the category of the "educated people" in this society.

G. Read the great Christian classics. These will help encourage your faith.

H. Read a good weekly news magazine and a good daily newspaper. This will help you keep abreast of what is happening now. Your local librarian or bookstore owner will help you find any of the aforementioned subjects.

Read and Grow!

Signing off From Barnes & Noble,

Daniel Whyte III

P.T.:

■　"A man who does not read good books has no

advantage over the man who can't read them."

—Unknown

- "Resolve to edge in a little reading every day. If you gain but 15 minutes a day, it will make itself felt at the end of a year."

—Horace Mann

- "When you know that you don't know, you've got to read."

—Solomon B. Fuller

- "Books began to happen to me."

—Langston Hughes

- "Temples fall, statues decay, mausoleums perish, eloquent phrases declaimed are forgotten, but good books are immortal."

—William T. Vernon

- "Books were my extended family."

—James Washington

THE IMPORTANCE OF INCREASING KNOWLEDGE

Letter Nine

Dear Y.B.M.:

I am writing this letter from the beautiful F.W. Bluford Library on the historically black North Carolina A & T University in Greensboro, North Carolina. I am in town for a special meeting that I am to speak at in a local church. But my being here in this particular library is quite fitting since in this letter I wish to encourage you to get a good education. This matter of getting a good education, or rather, increasing your knowledge, is extremely important — so important that even God addresses it in His Word: the Bible. Notice these words from the book of Proverbs 1:5:

"A wise man will hear and will increase learning; and a man of understanding shall attain unto wise counsels."

The value of getting a good education or "increasing your knowledge" is all around us. Notice just seven of the many advantages of "increasing your knowledge."

First, **through increasing your knowledge, you will receive personal enrichment and fulfillment.**

Second, **increasing your knowledge will give you a greater capacity to help others**.

Third, **getting a good education will, generally speaking, allow you throughout your life to do better financially and materially.**

Fourth, **increasing your knowledge will help you to deal with the vicissitudes of life better**.

Fifth, **increasing your knowledge will help you to interact with your family and other people better**.

Sixth, **getting a good education will allow you to better express yourself through speech and writing**.

Seventh, **increasing your knowledge can help you to become a more humble individual because you will find, as you increase in knowledge, how ignorant you really are**. Now, you may not think humility is a good quality to possess, but the fact of the matter is that you can't go up until you come down.

"The fear of the LORD is the instruction of wisdom; and before honour is humility."

—Proverbs 15:33

"Whosoever therefore shall humble himself as this little child, the same is greatest in the kingdom of heaven."

—Matthew 18:4

"Humble yourselves therefore under the mighty hand of God, that he may exalt you in due time."

—I Peter 5:6

The aforementioned advantages of getting a good education are just a few of the many advantages. There are many more. You will find them out as you increase your knowledge.

As I wrap this letter up, may I kindly but firmly say to you "CHANGE YOUR ATTITUDE TOWARD EDUCATION AND

KNOWLEDGE?" High school and college are not times to play! School time is not a time for partying! School is not a time for foolishness! School is serious business! Very serious business! Somebody somewhere is paying good money for you to obtain this knowledge. It is either your parents, some other member of your family, Mr. Tax-payer or yourself. This is not the time to be Mr. Cool! Change your attitude towards education, increase your knowledge and become a more powerful individual.

Do your best in High School, and get a good college education of some sort "**by any means necessary**."

For the Increasing of Knowledge,

Daniel

P.T.:

■   "A good head and a good heart are always a formidable combination."
—Nelson Mandela

■   "When we go into action and confront our adversaries, we must be as armed with as much knowledge as they."
—Dr. Martin Luther King, Jr.

■   "Real knowledge, properly used, will help anyone." —Romare Bearden

■   "Education is learning what you didn't even know you didn't know."
—Daniel J. Boorstin

71

- "Nothing pains some people more than having to think."

  —Dr. Martin Luther King, Jr.

- "The classroom is a sanctuary."

  —Daniel Whyte III

THE OBSTACLES TO GETTING A GOOD EDUCATION

Letter Ten

Dear Y.B.M.:

At this writing, I am on the steps of the Coleman Library on the campus of Florida A & M University in Tallahassee, Florida. I will be speaking in a couple of churches in the area on Sunday.

Frankly, I wish I had someone to write me like this when I was your age.

Now, on this important matter of getting a good college education: you will have some obstacles, to say the least.

The first obstacle that you will face is **yourself.** Why? Because the process of truly learning is laborious, monotonous, and at times down right bitter and boring. Therefore, obtaining a truly higher education will require of you a determined mind and a will to stick and stay. In short, it will take discipline. But in the end, it will be worth it all.

Your second obstacle to obtaining a higher education is the **ever present lure of immediate money and gratification**. This is a temptation. For example, you may have a good paying job right now and you don't want to leave it to go to college or you don't want to cut back on your hours so that you can go, at least, part-time. I recall, upon my graduation from high school, my parents wanted me to go on to college at Gardner-Webb College in North Carolina. However, I was too short-sighted, and, frankly, too foolish to take their advice because I had this restaurant job in high school that offered me a new job as trainer and assistant manager for new restaurants that were opening up. In my view, the money was good, so I opted for the fast money and the fast lifestyle of partying, women and drinking — immediate gratification. However, thankfully, by the grace of God, I came to my senses and began the higher learning process, and became a college graduate later.

My friend, you will learn in life that you must postpone gratification to reach for something far more important and valuable. One great preacher of the past put it this way:

> **You cannot offer up the future on the altar of the immediate.**

Of course, he is so right. I hope that you will learn this great lesson early instead of later.

A third obstacle that you will face will **be your friends.** Just as all men do not have faith, all men do not have knowledge, or wisdom or good sense. Just because your friends appear to be cool and powerful does not mean they have wisdom and good sense. If they are not increasing in knowledge, and if they are not exhorting you to do the same, then you are flying with the wrong birds. Get rid of them. Don't listen to them. Please don't let them keep you back from something as valuable as this.

The fourth obstacle will be **finding the right college**. Every college or university is not necessarily the right institution of higher learning for you. There are some colleges and universities that "teach you why." Then there are colleges and universities that "teach you how." And then there are colleges and universities that "teach you why and how." For the sake of common sense, please try to get into the college or university that can teach you the "why and the how."

A good way to determine whether or not a college is a "why or how" college is by examining the kind of people the college produces.

The students who come from the "why school" and the students who come from the "how school" will normally have the following characteristics:

They have that locked in, locked down mentality (commonly called the slave mentality.) This mentality is bent on working for somebody for thirty years, retiring, and then dying with nothing. In my opinion, these people do not carry the edge of what I call inside knowledge.

The students from the "why and how" college or university on the other hand, will normally have the following characteristics:

Independent thinkers, innovative, entrepreneurs; they may work for somebody for a little while, but their aim is to be in charge of their own business or what have you. These kind of folks will normally rise to the top more quickly than the rest of the pack. They will have their eyes on being free and doing their own thing. They have the inside scoop — the inside knowledge.

"Wisdom is the principal thing; therefore get wisdom: and with all thy getting get <u>understanding</u>."   —Proverbs 4:7

Your fifth obstacle, of course, will be the **money**. Please do not let the money problem strike fear into your heart because even in these days there are ways in which one can get an education, if he really wants to. Here are a few ways:

1. Prayer

2. Work part-time. Many have done it successfully.

3. Well-off family members.

4. External study colleges.

5. Junior or Community Colleges.

6. Scholarships for good grades

7. Financial Aid - Student Loans

And there are other options as well.

All I want to say to you in closing is this: I don't care what it takes, or how much it costs, please get yourself a good education. You will never regret it.

For a Smarter Young Black Man,

Daniel

P.T.:

■ "If you plan for a year, sow a seed;
If you plan for a decade, plant a tree
If you plan for a century, educate the people."
—Dr. Addie Mitchell
Professor, Morehouse College

■ "Education is the primary tool of emancipation and liberation for African-Americans in our fight for true equality in this country."

—Earl G. Graves

■ "Education is your passport to the future, for tomorrow belongs to the people who prepare for it today."

—Selected

■ "In the absence of education, all else fails."

—Governor Douglas Wilder

GRADUATING FROM COLLEGE AND STILL IGNORANT AND UNLEARNED

Letter Eleven

Dear Y.B.M.:

I trust that you are increasing in knowledge, understanding and wisdom.

I am writing this letter from Morehouse College in Atlanta, Georgia.

Now on the matter of education, I would like to kindly say to you, dear friend, please, please do not graduate from college ignorant, and sounding and looking uneducated.

To me, one of the most appalling things to see is a young man or woman for that matter, who has gone through four years of college and turned out to be just as dumb and ignorant as before he or she went in. I am forever amazed at people who have graduated from college, yet butcher the English language, come out with muddled thinking, and do not even know basic facts of history. For crying out loud, please do not come out of college like that. That is a waste of money and time.

How do people come out of a four-year institution of higher learning ignorant anyway? I believe it is because they go into college with the wrong idea of what college is for. Some go with no intentions on learning anything. These dear souls have nothing else to do, so they go to college with their buddies to pass the time and to carry on the same childish antics that they did in high school. And before they know it, the time that they wanted to pass passes away, and they barely graduate having cheated and skated their way through college, never having learned the very basics of a college education.

Sadly, often times, these dear souls come out of college throwing down the same old foolishness they were throwing down before they went to college. Then they want a Fortune 500 Company to hire them on. And when they fail a simple test to get an entry-level position, they cry racism. How ridiculous!

Dear Y.B.M., if you have the opportunity to go to college, go to college to learn something — not to play.

Yours For Learning Something,

Daniel

P.T.:

■ "We cannot afford to settle for being just average; we must learn as much as we can to be the best that we can. The key word is education - that's knowledge — education with maximum effort."
—Bill Cosby

■ "My brain is the key to set me free."
—Harry Houdini

■ "The mind is a terrible thing to waste."
—Slogan, Negro College Fund

■ "The best possible investment you can make in your future is an education. Even if you default on your student loan, nobody can repossess your diploma." —Steven Silbiger, author, *The Jewish Phenomenon*

THE MARKS OF A TRULY EDUCATED MAN

Letter Twelve

Dear Y.B.M.:

This letter is being written from the beautiful Kellogg Conference Center on the campus of Tuskegee University in Tuskegee, Alabama.

If you are an upwardly mobile individual, you may have wondered from time to time, how does one know that he is educated? In other words, what are the marks of an educated man?

Here are some of the marks that I have observed about truly knowledgeable people or those considered truly educated:

First, **they have a healthy and humble respect and reverence for Almighty God**. This principle of an educated man is found in the Book of Wisdom, which is the book of Proverbs in the Holy Bible. The verse reads:

"The fear of the Lord is the beginning of knowledge."

A person who does not acknowledge and reverence God Almighty is not considered a wise or educated man. In fact, God considers him a fool. "He is ignorant and knoweth nothing." No matter how many years of schooling he has behind him, if he does not recognize and respect and fear Almighty God, he is a fool according to the Word of God.

"The fool hath said in his heart, There is no God."
—Psalm 14:1a

There is an old negro saying that also comes to mind here:

"Education without salvation is damnation."

The other day I saw a very striking sign at a church. It read:

> **The dead atheist**
> **The dead agnostic**
> **and the dead saint**
> **All believe God exists now.**

A second **mark of an educated man is that he is humble enough to admit his ignorance**. He realizes that no matter how much he learns, he will never learn or know everything.

Third, **a truly educated man continues his education long after his years in high school and college**. He learns until he dies. In the words of Quincy Jones: "He grows until he goes."

Another mark of a truly educated man is that he is authentic. He is an original. He is for real. He is himself. He knows he does not have to be like anyone else. He is therefore original in his thinking, his speaking, and his writing. An educated man is normally very comfortable with himself as well as with others. One commentator uses this phrase: "He is comfortable in his own skin." I like it.

Another mark of an educated man is that he uses his education and knowledge for wise and good purposes. Of course, he uses it to generate a living for himself and his family. But not only for that, he also uses it to help others who are less fortunate than himself.

Sixth, **to me, one of the greatest marks of an educated man is** the ability to express himself clearly through his speech and through his writing.

Then, **an educated man is a disciplined man**. A disciplined man is willing and able to "do the worst first." He is willing and ready to tackle the difficult jobs and tasks even when he does not feel like doing them.

Eighth, **the educated man exudes an inexplicable quiet confidence about himself**. He is not loud, boisterous or arrogant. But you somehow get the feeling that he knows what he is doing. He normally does not say much, but you somehow sense that if he does say something, it would be more important and weighty than what most people have to say.

Ninth, **the educated man is not a perfect man, but he strives to be a moral man.** He has a strong sense of what is right and wrong. And it is his aim to do the right thing. Because of this, he normally finds favor in the sight of God and man.

Finally, **another mark of an educated man is that he understands etiquette and protocol**. In other words, not only is he smart; he knows how to look smart as well. He knows what to say in different settings. He knows how to act at a backyard barbecue as well as at a stately dinner. He dresses and acts appropriately on any given occasion.

Dear Y.B.M., I strongly suggest that you strive to be this kind of man.

For The Educated Black Man,

Daniel

P.T.:

■ "It is part of the function of education to help us escape - not from our own time, for we are bound by that - but from the intellectual and emotional limitations of our own time."

—T. S. Eliot, poet

■ "Education is an ornament in prosperity and a refuge in adversity."

—Aristotle, philosopher

■ "Nothing is more important than a good education."

—Roy Wilkins

■ "Without education you are not going anywhere in this world. Education is the passport to our future."

—Selected

■ "He who opens a school door, closes a prison."

—Victor Hugo

■ "Human history becomes more and more a race between education and catastrophe."

—H. G. Wells

WITH ALL THY GETTING, GET WISDOM AND UNDERSTANDING

Letter Thirteen

Dear Y.B.M.:

I trust that you are growing.

As I have shared with you in previous letters, it is true that gaining more education and acquiring knowledge is very important and essential to your success as we know it in this life. However, let me quickly say to you that there is something more important than these things, and that is obtaining WISDOM. While you are gaining more knowledge, please also get wisdom.

Notice what King Solomon said:

"Wisdom is the principal thing; therefore get wisdom: and with all thy getting get understanding."
—Proverbs 4:7

What is wisdom? The word "wisdom" literally means having skill. Education will tell you how to do something, but wisdom will tell you why you ought to do something. And wisdom will also tell you when you ought to do something. In other words, knowledge or education is the automobile, but wisdom is the fuel. Wisdom is that supernatural edge that most people do not have, and have no idea how to get. King Solomon, the wisest man who ever lived, said: Wisdom is more valuable than gold, silver and rubies. In fact, if you don't have wisdom, you won't have and certainly won't keep much gold, silver and rubies.

Probably, besides my letter on "Get to Know Your Creator" (Letter Two), this short letter is the most important to your happiness, success, and advancement in this life.

Now very simply, here is the basic way to obtain true wisdom. But watch out: this is going to be so simple that you might miss it.

ASK GOD FOR IT!

That's right. If you want true wisdom, you must simply ask God for it. You cannot work for wisdom; you cannot study and get wisdom; you cannot borrow wisdom; you cannot buy wisdom; and you cannot extract wisdom from other human beings. The only way to get true wisdom is by simply praying and asking God for it. It is a free gift of the grace of God, as is your soul's salvation.

"If any of you lack wisdom, let him ask of God, that giveth to all men liberally, and upbraideth not; and it shall be given him."

—James 1:5

The glorious wisdom that God gives will open your eyes to so many things that you cannot see right now. The wisdom of God will give you the ability to see things that the average person does not see. Having the wisdom of God will also definitely give you an advantage — a great advantage in this life. So I urge you to ask God for wisdom to guide you throughout your life, and, friend, He will do it for you.

In closing this letter, let me also say that if you want to be wise, it is wise to walk or hang with wise men. King Solomon said:

"He that walketh with wise men shall be wise, but a

companion of fools shall be destroyed."   —Proverbs 13:20

Dear Y.B.M., even though it feels good and may look cool, please don't hang with fools because if you do, you will eventually become a fool yourself. Pick out those guys who are wise and hang with them and be a wise guy yourself.

"Wisdom is the principal thing; therefore get wisdom: and with all thy getting get understanding."

—Proverbs 4:7

A Word To The Wise,

Daniel

P.T.:

■ "The world belongs to the man who is wise enough to change his mind in the presence of facts."

—Roy L. Smith

■ "Patience is bitter but its fruit is sweet."

—Jean Jacques Rousseau

■ "Gentlemen, try not to become men of success. Rather, become men of value."

—Albert Einstein

■ "Perhaps the most valuable result of all education is the ability to make yourself do the thing you have to do, when it ought to be done, whether you like it or not."

—T. H.

PLEASE LEARN "YOURSELF" A LITTLE ETIQUETTE

Letter Fourteen

Dear Y.B.M.:

In this letter, I wish to encourage you to do something that is very important and that is crucial to your advancement in whatever field you enter into. Also, if you learn the principles of this subject, you will gain great peace of mind when dealing with people.

Here is what I want to encourage you to do: Learn "yourself" some etiquette.

Personally, I believe that etiquette is the capstone of a man's education. For one should not only be smart in his head, but one should also be smart in how he relates to other people. A truly educated man certainly knows what he knows, but he also knows how to act in every given situation or occasion. Sadly, many schools do not spend much time on this very important subject.

What is etiquette anyway? According to the *Random House Dictionary of the English Language* — etiquette is:

> **Conventional requirements as to social behaviour, proprieties of conduct as established in any class or community or for any occasion.**

> **A prescribed or accepted code of usage in matters of ceremony as at a court or official or other formal observances.**

My definition of etiquette is: doing that which is right, proper, polite and kind in dealing with our fellow human beings.

Unfortunately, most of us have never taken a course in etiquette. And very few parents have taken the time to teach their children the basic principles of good etiquette. If you are one of the millions who have not been taught, take heart! Below is a list of quality books that you can read and study so that you can educate yourself as to what to do when the time presents itself. You will not need to read the entire list, but, at least read one of these books or maybe even two. Also, get a small paperback book on the subject that you can keep close at hand, as a quick reference.

Here we go. Below are the top six books on the subject of etiquette:

The Amy Vanderbuilt
Complete Book of Etiquette
Revised and Expanded
By Letitia Baldrige
(Doubleday & Company)

A Gentleman at The Table: A Concise, Contemporary
Guide to Table Manners
John Bridges & Bryan Curtis
(Rutledge Hill Press)

Miss Manners'
Guide To Excruciatingly Correct Behaviour
By Judith Martin
(Atheneum)

How To Be A Gentleman: A Contemporary Guide to Common Courtesy
John Bridges
(Rutledge Hill Press)

The Correct Thing: A Guide Book of Etiquette for Young Men
Alyce Derian
(Author House)

The New Emily Post's Etiquette
By Elizabeth L. Post

I do not agree with everything in any of the books listed above, but any one of these books will help you get on the right track as to how to act.

Now, out of all of the books listed above, I would recommend your reading the one by Emily Post. I really like the down-to-earth tone of the book, as well as the humor of it.

In closing, my brother, let me say, please don't get carried away with this etiquette stuff. Just learn the basic rules of how to carry yourself well and then be natural. And remember: keep it real!

Yours For Not Only Being Smart, But Looking Smart,

Daniel

P.T.:

■   "Do a common thing in an uncommon way."
—Booker T. Washington

■ "Thinking your way through your problem is better than wishing your way through."

—Coleman Young

■ "Create and be true to yourself, and depend only on your own good taste."

—Duke Ellington

ON YOUR LIFE — AS A YOUNG BLACK MAN

YOU ARE NOT INFERIOR!

Letter Fifteen

Dear Y.B.M.:

I am back in Atlanta, and at the writing of this letter, I am on the beautiful campus of Morehouse College — the alma mater of the late and great Dr. Martin Luther King, Jr.

Down through the years, I have noticed that one of the marks of a "Morehouse man" is confidence. And that is what I want to write to you about today.

I hope that you are not one of the many young men in our community who feels inferior and shows that he feels inferior to other races — particularly the white race. It is disturbing to see so many young black men catch this disease called an inferiority complex when it comes to other races. It is almost as though this disease is in the air in the black community.

What are some of the ways that we catch this awful disease? Well, **one way to get this disease is by not being raised right**. Often times, if a parent does not know how to love and nurture a child while he is young, especially black boys, that child will grow up out of balance mentally, therefore feeling inferior. I am one of those who believe that young black children need lots of love, nurturing, and encouragement to turn out right in this strange society that we live in, especially black boys. It is crucial.

I believe the second reason why young black men feel inferior to others is **because they have become addicted to that one eyed monster - the television set**. I am convinced through my own observation of children that those children who grow up with a heavy diet of television watching will often times end up with feelings of inferiority. This happens simply because they are constantly watching others on the tube doing things and who are progressing and moving forward with their lives while they just watch. Of course, most of the people we see on television are white, and certainly most of the people we see in positive roles on television are white. This constant bombardment on our young black boys is destructive. One of the reasons why I don't let my children watch television is because I don't want them to think that white people are the standard of beauty and I don't want them to think that white is always right.

In consequence of this heavy dose of television watching, they never develop a pattern of progress and success for their own lives, thus making their lives feel and appear inferior. The more you conquer, succeed, and prosper, the more competent and confident you will become.

A third reason for this feeling of inferiority among young black men **is because many do not pursue more knowledge.** I didn't say education. Unfortunately, knowledge and education are not necessarily the same in our society. Be that as it may, the more knowledge that you have, the more confidence you will have. It is trite, but true – KNOWLEDGE IS POWER — and, may I say, huge power. Knowledge puts a smile on your face and a pep in your step that is unmistakable. Now when I speak of knowledge and confidence, I don't speak of this haughty, snobbish and proud attitude that can come with knowledge. For Saint Paul said it well: *"Knowledge puffeth up, but charity edifieth"* (I Corinthians 8:1). No, I am speaking of the humble gaining of bold, loving, and biblical confidence.

No matter where we come from, what side of the tracks we live on, how rich or poor, we as young black men can and must have the confidence and boldness to accomplish great things that God designed for us to do.

Out of all of the billions of folks who have been born into this world, there is no one like you; and there is no one who can do what you can do.

No one is better than you. You
are just as good as anyone else,

Daniel

P.T.:

- "I did not equate my self-worth with my wins and losses." —Arthur Ashe

- "The most important thing I have to fight as a black person in an oppressive, racist society is what I think about myself." —Mark Mathabane

- "With a spirit straining toward true self-esteem, the Negro must boldly throw off the manacles of self-abnegation and say to himself and the world: 'I am somebody. I am a person. I am a man with dignity and honor. I have a rich and noble history.'" —Dr. Martin Luther King, Jr.

- "If you respect yourself, it's easier to respect other people. —John Singleton

■ "I think one of my basic flaws has been a lack of self-esteem...always feeling like I had to do more. I never could do enough or be good enough."

—Max Robinson

TAKE THE ROAD LESS TRAVELED

Letter Sixteen

Dear Y.B.M.:

I trust that you are doing well today.

I am writing you now to encourage you to take the "road less traveled." You might be asking, what is the road less traveled? Well, in short, it is the tough, lonely road of self-discipline. This road is about delaying gratification and pleasure to accomplish a worthy goal or pursuit. Practicing discipline is much easier said than done. Discipline is a great idea, but implementing it is difficult.

According to *Websters Collegiate Dictionary*, the word ***discipline*** means:

> -To bring under control
> -Training that corrects, molds or perfects the mental faculties or moral character
> -Self control
> -To train or develop by instruction and exercise especially in self-control
> -Control gained by enforcing obedience or order

Discipline is that quality that says, by the grace of God, come hell or high water, I am determined to get the task done or reach that goal, etc. Discipline says, it doesn't matter how I feel or what is going on around me or who is doing or saying what. All that matters is that I am willing to sacrifice – to do without things, if necessary, to reach my goal.

Here is a personal example of self-discipline: to write this book, I've had to get up at 3:30 a.m., forego eating, get rid of the television set, and not look at football and basketball, etc.

Dear friend, you will have to have that rugged tenacity and discipline if you are going to succeed in your endeavours in this life.

Here are some things that we really need to practice the principle of discipline in:

PRAYER: You will need to learn to pray when you feel like praying and pray even when you don't.

READING: Especially Bible reading. One man said: "The Bible will keep you away from sin, or sin will keep you away from the Bible." Reading other books besides the Bible will take discipline as well. But the rewards are great.

IN-DEPTH STUDY: King Solomon, the wisest man that ever lived, said, *"Much study is a weariness of the flesh"* (Ecclesiastes 12:12b). And it is. Someone stated that "Mental work is much more difficult than physical work." And that is true. For example, I find it much easier to work in a warehouse than to sit down and write an article or a book.

EXERCISE: Even though there are people who say they like to exercise, it still takes discipline to move that body out of bed and on to the running track or gym. Discipline! Discipline! Discipline! Make it your battle cry and you will win every time.

SEX: One of the most difficult areas to exercise discipline in is the area of sexual desires. But as in any thing else, God will help you overcome those temptations if you would only pray and take heed to His Word.

We could go on and on as to the areas we need to practice discipline in. The question now is, how do we practice discipline? Here are some simple ideas that I find helpful:

1. When you have a goal that needs to be reached, abandon all else and **<u>focus</u>** on that one thing that needs to be done and get it done now!

2. Take the T.V. out of the house.

3. Do the worst first.

4. Work hard and then have big fun. Plan an exciting reward for yourself after the goal is reached.

5. Remember that good feelings follow positive action. Positive action hardly ever follows good feelings.

6. Fast. When you really have to get something done, do what I call, **fast and focus**. What I mean by this is in order to reach your goal, you may need to go without some things that you enjoy such as food or television for a period of time to focus on accomplishing your goal.

7. Bathe the goal or project in prayer.

Dear Y.B.M., please take the road less traveled — the road of discipline. It's hard, but good. And as my dad used to say: "It's tight, but right!"

On the Road Less Traveled,

Daniel Whyte

P.T.:

- "The collapse of character begins with compromise."
  —Frederick Douglass

- "When you do the things you have to do when you have to do them, the day will come when you can do the things you want to do when you want to do them."
  —Zig Ziglar

- "If you can force your heart and nerve and sinew
  To serve your turn long after they are gone,
  And so hold on when there is nothing in you
  Except the Will which says to them: 'Hold on.'

  "If you can fill the unforgiving minute
  With sixty seconds' worth of distance run-
  Yours is the Earth and everything that's in it,
  And- which is more - you'll be a Man, my son!"
  —Rudyard Kipling

TAKE FULL RESPONSIBILITY

Letter Seventeen

Dear Y.B.M.:

I am writing you today from a basement office of a church in New Haven, Connecticut. I trust that you are continuing to grow as a young man.

In this letter, I would like to kindly share with you some things about taking responsibility for yourself, and for your life. Somehow, many of us, as young black men, did not acquire a healthy attitude towards self-responsibility. Frankly, many of us are afraid of responsibility. Obviously, there are some who are not afraid of responsibility. But many of us are. And the lack of this one quality can handicap you throughout your life.

I believe that the main reason why many of us as young black men do not have a healthy attitude towards self-responsibility **is because we have never been taught it, and because, we have not seen it exemplified by many older black men.** Most of us have seen our black women take responsibility, but seldom have we seen our black men do so. This is a tragedy.

The quality of taking responsibility does not come naturally. It has to be taught — more by example than by anything else.

A second reason why we do not take responsibility for our lives as we should **is because self-responsibility goes against human nature.** Taking responsibility does not come easy. It is human nature, and much easier to be irresponsible than responsible. It is easier, but not better, to have the attitude that the world owes you

103

something — when it does not! It is easier, but not better, to let others take care of you. It is easier, but not better, to be an employee and not the boss. (Believe it or not, being the boss is much more difficult than being the employee. Why? Because the boss is responsible for everything.) It is much easier, but not necessarily better, to stay single even if you do not have the gift of celibacy, than to get married. But staying single and having sex and having babies is irresponsible as well as destructive to so many lives including your own. It is far better to make a commitment to someone special, be responsible, get married, have children, and take care of your family. And may I say being married with children takes a mature and responsible person.

Now below are some of the dangers of not taking responsibility for ourselves and our lives:

1. You will live a sad life, constantly having to blame others for your failures and problems. But this will just make matters worse. The problem, son, is "the man in the mirror."

2. You will live a life of constantly being a follower and not a leader, because a leader must take responsibility for himself and others.

3. You will live a pathetic life, constantly depending on other people.

You may not be a completely responsible person now, but the good news is that you can be. Here is the main way that you and I can do that:

By simply making a firm resolute DECISION to be responsible for yourself, your life and for those God places under your care. Always remember that much of life is a matter of decisions. Whatever you are, whatever you are doing, and whatever you become, will rest largely upon the decisions that you make in life. Not only is "knowledge power," but "decision is power" as well. Decisions are powerful for good or bad. At every issue in life, and at every crossroad, take the high road of self-responsibility.

If you need more money, get a job. No excuses! Just get a job. Don't have car insurance? The law requires that you have it. Get the insurance or stop driving. A bill is due? Either pay it or call the people and make other arrangements. No excuses! Just do it! Have you found the right lady that God wants you to marry? Don't shirk! Don't jive! Don't hee-haw and mee-maw! Take responsibility and marry the girl, and then take responsibility and take care of her and the children. No excuses! Just do the right thing.

Take responsibility for all that you do, all that you say and all that you are, and never blame anyone else for your situation.

Taking Responsibility,

Daniel Whyte

P.T.:

■ "Success is the result of hard work, learning from failure, loyalty, and persistence."
—Colin L. Powell

■ "Image is what people think we are; integrity is what we really are."
—John Maxwell

■ "Integrity is the glue that holds our way of life together. We must constantly strive to keep our

105

integrity intact. When wealth is lost, nothing is lost; when health is lost, something is lost; when character is lost, all is lost."

—Billy Graham

TALK AND LISTEN TO EVERY OLDER BLACK MAN PAST FIFTY THAT YOU POSSIBLY CAN

Letter Eighteen

Dear Y.B.M.:

I realize that you may feel more comfortable with those who are of the same age as you. However, may I suggest to you that it is very important that you spend some quality time talking to and listening to every older black man past fifty that you possibly can? These men will not claim perfection, nor will they claim to have it all together. Many of them will not have the educational background that you may have. But it behooves you to be quiet and listen to them.

Dear friend, because of the light that you have received in this age of knowledge and information, you may know a little about the super highways of life; but you don't know much, if anything, about the smaller back-roads and shortcuts of life. Also, even though you may know a little about the main highways of life, you do not know what lies ahead on those highways. These older gentlemen do, because they have passed this way before. There is a lot that you think you know that you don't know. As you grow older you will become increasingly aware of how ignorant you really are. These dear older brothers, who have passed this way before, have been down both the super highways and the small back-roads and shortcuts. And they can really help you make a grand success of this life, if you would only listen to them. For as the Bible says:

"The fear of the Lord is the beginning of knowledge: but fools despise wisdom and instruction."
—Proverbs 1:7

"Where no counsel is, the people fall: but in the multitude of counselors there is safety."

—Proverbs 11:14

Here are some of the wonderful and positive things that older men can impart to you if you are ready to hear a "word to the wise."

1. They can help you avoid the pitfalls along the road of life.

2. They can outline for you the priorities in life that you need to concentrate on.

3. They can advise you as to which road is best for you to take at various junctions on the road of life.

4. The real good, older men will admit their mistakes and failures, and will genuinely try to help you to avoid them.

Listen, learn and live, dear brother.

Now most of these wise older brothers will let it be known that they do not have time to waste. Nor do they like to offer their valuable advice and time to just anybody — particularly one who is a fool. (i.e., one who will not listen to and heed sound advice.) So, these wise, old men are not called wise, old men for nothing. They can see right through you. They know if you are sincere or not. They will be slow and cautious in dealing with you until they are convinced you are for real. Now here are some ways to convince them that you are sincere:

1. **Do not act in any way as though you already know the answer to all of the various issues of life**. (Even if you do know, don't act as though you do.) The fact of the matter is,

YOU DO NOT KNOW ALL THAT YOU THINK YOU KNOW! So, don't be a "know it all." Shut up! while the man is talking, and please do not say stupid things like "I already know that." Listen. Really listen. If these men detect that you are not really listening to them, they will not tell you anything.

2. **Ask intelligent questions, and wait for the answer**. If he does not give you the answer, then ask again. Re-phrase the question. Do what you have to do to get the answer. Bug them, bother them, annoy them. It is that important. Sometimes you have to dig for gold, son.

3. **Don't waste their time**. Be very concerned about their time. They will appreciate it. Their time is more important than yours, not only because of their age, but because their time is shorter. Usually men, fifty and above, don't play around anymore when it comes to their time. They are very serious about their time, and you had better be too, or they will abruptly cut you off.

Think your questions through. Write your questions down. Do not go in half-cocked.

4. **Train yourself to spend more time around older, wise men, than young, foolish men**. (There are some young, wise men too, by the way, but not many.) Young, foolish men can't teach you anything; older, wise men can teach you a lot. If you want to become a better, wiser man, hang with the heavies.

Most of my close friends are at least ten years my senior. Their age, wisdom, advice and encouragement has been of great benefit and blessing to me. Through their wise counsel, I have avoided many pitfalls and have received some bread to pass on to my younger brothers. I hope that you will take my advice and start listening to the older, wiser brothers.

Hanging With The Heavies,

Daniel

P.T.:

■ "A person completely wrapped up in himself makes a small package."
—Denzel Washington

■ "Truth is proper and beautiful in all times and in all places."
—Frederick Douglass

■ "A true friend never gets in your way unless you happen to be going down."
—Arnold H. Glasgow

■ "Align yourself with powerful people. Align yourself with people that you can learn from, people who want more out of life, people who are stretching and searching and seeking some higher ground in life."
—Les Brown

■ "A friend may well be reckoned the masterpiece of nature."
—Ralph Waldo Emerson

LEARN ABOUT WHERE YOU COME FROM

Letter Nineteen

Dear Y.B.M.:

I trust that you are doing well today.

This is just a short letter to encourage you to learn more about your heritage and where you came from. This is more important than you may think. It is crucial to your self-esteem, confidence and vision for the future. You see, having knowledge of your history will help make you a wiser person today, and give you a better idea as to where to go in the future. As they say, a person who does not know where he came from does not know where he is going.

Now, this important knowledge is gained in two basic ways: One way is by word of mouth: i.e., through the words of parents, aunts, uncles, grandparents and great grandparents. And, of course, the second way is through reading and studying good black history books.

In my last letter, I exhorted you to speak to older black men in general. In this letter, I want to encourage you to take some time and visit your older relatives, and ask them some questions about how it was "back when." Ask questions like, what did they go through? How did they handle racism? What were my ancestors like? Where did they live? What did they do? What kind of personalities did they have? What made them what they were? What interests, desires and dreams did they have? Dear Y.B.M., you can learn a great deal about yourself by learning about your people. You can learn from their successes as well as their failures and mistakes.

Earlier, I also mentioned the value of books in this regard. Simply put, it would help you greatly to read two or three Black American history books as well as history books on Africa and two or three general American history books. If you read, study, and absorb such books, you will be head and shoulders above the crowd as far as how to handle present situations and people, and as to how to plan for the future.

A good working knowledge of history is crucial. By taking heed of this humble advice, you will gain a perspective on life that is rare among young people today. It will give you a proper perspective on your role and place in America and the world. With this knowledge, you will be able to more successfully relate to your own people as well as to others.

> **Those who cannot remember the past are condemned to repeat it.**
> —George Santayana

Go back, son, so you can go forward.

Going Back,

Daniel

P.T.:

■ "It is impossible to love ourselves without having an affection for Africa."   —Randall Robinson

■ "Our Black heritage must be a foundation stone we can build on, not a place to withdraw to."
—Colin L. Powell

■ "We build our temples for tomorrow, strong as we know how, and we stand on top of the mountain, free within ourselves."

—Langston Hughes

■ "Let us hold up our heads and with firm and steady tread go manfully forward."

—Booker T. Washington

■ "We must give our children a sense of pride in being Black. The glory of our past and the dignity of our present must lead the way to the power of our future."

—Adam Clayton Powell, Jr.

■ "I can move between different disciplines because I am essentially a storyteller, and the story I want to tell is about black people. I always want to share my great satisfaction at being a black man at this time in history."

—Ossie Davis

THE VALUE OF WORKING HARD AND SMART

Letter Twenty

Dear Y.B.M.:

I do not want to sound like I am preaching to you, but to start this important letter, I must ask you to please take note of the following verses from the Book of books:

"The desire of the slothful killeth him; for his hands refuse to labour."

—Solomon from
Proverbs 21:25

"The soul of the sluggard desireth, and hath nothing: but the soul of the diligent shall be made fat."

—Solomon from
Proverbs 13:4

"He becometh poor that dealeth with a slack hand: but the hand of the diligent maketh rich."

—Solomon from
Proverbs 10:4

Those old proverbs above are true, and you can see the truth of these verses all around you. Those who choose to be lazy and slothful with their lives usually end up poor and dependent upon others; while those who make up their minds to work diligently end up having the things that they need, and also many of the good things that they desire.

Based upon these truths, I want to strongly encourage you to be determined to not be a lazy person, but rather a person who will learn to love work, and one who will work consistently and diligently.

Now, how does a person become slothful and lazy in the first place?

First, **a person can become lazy because it is a natural tendency of mankind to avoid work and that which is difficult or that which appears difficult**. Unfortunately, it is a part of our sinful nature as human beings to be lazy.

Second, **many young men today are raised to be lazy** — not intentionally, I am sure, but the result is the same. Well-meaning parents who attempt to give their dear children "a better life than they had" have a tendency to not teach their children the value and importance of hard work and labor and the proverbial "value of a dollar." These dear, well-meaning parents, have a tendency to just give the child everything he wants without that child working for anything and earning it the "old fashioned way." Therefore, the poor child grows up to be a man with the pitiful notion in his mind that the world owes him something for free. And in real life, it doesn't work that way.

I believe a third reason why so many young men become lazy is **because of their addiction to television and this new thing called the video game**. Too many of our young black men spend too much time before the television set watching others do their thing and make their money, while they do nothing. On top of that, much television watching gives young men a warped sense of what real life is about. Most of television is fiction and we cannot continue to live fiction lives in a non-fiction world. Get this: TV is not reality! TV is not reality! TV is not reality! Even "reality TV" is not reality! Please stop watching others accomplish things and accomplish something yourself.

Here are some good ways that you can break the slothfulness habit if you struggle with this universal problem.

1. Sit down and define what you are about and what it is you would like to accomplish in life. Set specific goals and pursue them.

2. Make up a time schedule and plan how you will achieve your goals. And then pursue them like a mad man.

3. Be determined with the tenacity of a Bulldog, that you will not let anyone or anything get in your way of doing what you know you ought to do.

4. Get into the habit of going to bed earlier and getting up earlier. Most people can accomplish more in a given day simply by getting up by 5:00 a.m. as opposed to 8:00 a.m. or 9:00 a.m. Try it before you think I am nuts.

5. Work your plan! Work your plan! Work your plan! And work it daily. Never, never quit no matter what happens.

Dear brother, if you desire a college education, then you will have to work for it. If you desire to start a business, then you will have to work for it. If you desire to write a book, you will have to work. If you desire the "finer things in life," you will have to work for them. Hard work pays great dividends. As Saint Paul said:

"For even when we were with you, this we commanded you, that if any would not work, neither should he eat."
—II Thessalonians 3:10

Now, that's serious.

Working,

Daniel

P.T.:

- "When you are laboring for others let it be with the same zeal as if it were for yourself."
  —Unknown

- "The secret to success is to learn to accept the impossible, to do without the indispensable, and to bear the intolerable."
  —Nelson Mandela

- "If it falls your lot to be a street sweeper, sweep streets as Raphael painted pictures, sweep streets as Michelangelo carved marble, sweep streets as Beethoven composed music, or Shakespeare wrote poetry."
  —Dr. Martin Luther King, Jr.

- "Everything comes to him who hustles while he waits."
  —Thomas A. Edison

THINGS I WISH SOMEONE HAD TOLD ME WHEN I WAS TWELVE

Letter Twenty-One

Dear Y.B.M.:

Today, I would like to share with you some things that I wish someone had forcibly told me when I was twelve years old. Sadly, some of the things that I am going to mention in this letter, I learned at H.K.C. — Hard Knocks College. And that is not the college to go to. Indeed, it is the college from hell. I hope that you will allow me to now be that sign post of wisdom I wish I had when I was your age. If you take heed of what I am going to say here, it will save you many heartaches and troubles.

First of all, **I wish someone had seriously taken the Bible and plainly showed me what true salvation really meant when I was younger, as I showed you in Letter Two**. True salvation in my earlier life would have made a big difference in my life as it will yours. Accept the Lord Jesus Christ as your Saviour as soon as you can.

Second, **I wish someone had told me about the importance of reading, studying and applying the Bible to my life**. Read, study and apply the Bible to your life, and be the success that God wants you to be.

Third, **I wish someone had forcibly told me to avoid having sex until after I was married**. And I wish they had told me the Biblical reasons why. I know that it sounds weird and foreign, but Y.B.M., avoid having sex of any kind until after you are married.

Here is just one verse from God's Word that gives you a reason why:

"Flee fornication. Every sin that a man doeth is without the body; but he that committeth fornication sinneth against his own body."

—I Corinthians 6:18

Fourth, **I wish someone had taught me about the proverbial "value of a dollar."** In other words, I wish someone had taught me how to manage money better, and how to save and invest it as well.

Money is not everything, but money is important. In fact the Bible says, *"Money answereth all things"* (Ecclesiastes 10:9). And the way you handle it will be one of the keys to your success. So if you don't know how to handle your money, get with a good businessman and learn all that you can about how to make, handle, and invest money. I will write you another letter about money in the near future.

Fifth, **I wish that someone had taught me how to manage my time better**. I wish I had learned the value of each minute of life at an earlier age. Time is like money – we must spend it wisely. Do whatever it takes to learn how to manage the time that God gives you.

Sixth, **I wish that someone had taught me to have a better work ethic**. There is nothing wrong with hard work. Hard work is the road to lasting success. Learn to see work as a friend and not an enemy. Work hard and smart.

Seventh, **I wish that someone had told me, in a forcible manner,**

that junior high school and high school were not times in which to play, but to gain knowledge. I wish someone had told me that school and learning were a priviledge and not something to be despised.

Eighth, **I wish someone had told me that life was not going to always be easy, and that I needed to take life more seriously because this is the only life I get**.

Ninth, **I wish someone had told me that just because we had integration in our schools, racism and prejudice did not end**.

Tenth, **I wish someone had forcibly told me not to hang around the wrong crowd** — that it was not cool — but rather, to be independent and to think for myself and to do that which was right "though the stars fall."

In my writing about what I wished someone had told me when I was younger, I have in turn told you some things that if you were to take heed of, would save you many a hard knocks.

Do the right thing and "make Black America better."

Yours For Not Going To H.K.C.,

Daniel

P.T.:

■ "I have learnt that success is to be measured not so much by the position that one has reached in life as by the obstacles which he has overcome while trying to succeed."
—Booker T. Washington

■ "Our greatest glory is not in never falling, but in rising every time we fall."

—Confucius

■ "America's massive social breakdown requires that we come together — for the sake of our lives, our children, and our sacred honor."

—Cornel West

■ "When you do the common things in life in an uncommon way, you will command the attention of the world."

—George Washington Carver

■ "Nobody, but nobody can make it out here alone."

—Maya Angelou

HOW TO BE REALLY COOL

Letter Twenty-two

Dear Y.B.M.:

I trust that you are a cool fellow.

In this letter, I would like to mention some things on this matter of "being cool." Now you may think it strange that I am writing on the subject of being cool in a book of this nature. But, in my opinion, being cool is important. In fact, being cool is a cool thing to do.

What coolness is not...

Now being cool is not necessarily wearing your cap on backwards, or having your pants hanging off your tail. Coolness is not necessarily having an N.B.A. jacket on twice your size. Coolness is not having three or four girlfriends and having babies by each of them. Being cool is not smoking, drinking and doing drugs. Coolness is not carrying a gun or being a part of a gang. It is not skipping school to hang with the boys. Friend of mine, I am not merely suggesting that these things are not cool. I know these things are not cool. Get away from foolishness and learn how to be really cool.

So what is real coolness?

Real coolness in my book is being prepared so that you will never look un-cool. Real coolness is being un-ruffled at the various vicissitudes of life. Brother-Friend, real coolness is that quiet confidence in knowing that God is in control and knowing that everything will be alright. Coolness is having inexplicable peace, joy and calmness even in the midst of the storms of life. God calls

123

this peace and joy *"Peace that passeth all understanding"* (Philippians 4:7), and *"joy unspeakable"* (I Peter 1:8). To me, being cool is also being able to express yourself clearly even when you are under fire. Being cool is being able to keep your tongue under control even from defending yourself from the accusations of fools.

In closing, let me say that coolness is knowing what to do, how to do it, and when to do it.

Are you really "cool," friend? Or do you just look cool?

Yours For Never Letting Them See You Sweat,

Daniel

P.T.:

■   "The secret of success is to be like a duck - smooth and unruffled on top, but paddling furiously underneath."

—Unknown

WOMEN FOLK!

Letter Twenty-three

Dear Y.B.M.:

This letter will probably be the most controversial letter that I write you. However, I hope that you read it and take heed to it.

In this letter, I want to talk to you about one of the most important issues in life for the young black man or any man for that matter, and that is his relationship with the women folk. The older you get, the more you will realize how important it is to understand how to deal with women. A good woman can help you become a great success in life; a bad woman can not only make your life miserable, but she can ruin your life as well. It is as simple as that. Notice what the wisest man who ever lived said:

"A virtuous woman is a crown to her husband: but she that maketh ashamed is as rottenness in his bones."
—Proverbs 12:4

"For a whore is a deep ditch; and a strange woman is a narrow pit."
—Proverbs 23:27

My dear brother, there are some things that you need to know about dealing with women folk that will help you avoid much trouble and sorrow, and that will help you find the right woman as your life's mate. The following are some things that you will want to keep in mind as you deal with the women folk:

1. **Understand that women are designed by God to be a help and a blessing to man, not a hinderance**.

2. **Think with your big head; not with your little head**. In other words, don't let your life be driven by sex, but rather by God's Word, and what is right. Too many young and old men today love sex more than they love God. My old school fellows and I used to call men like this "sex-whipped." Well, it was a little bit more graphic than that, but I can't go there here.

3. **Everything that glitters ain't gold**. It is a tragedy, but true, that most pretty and fine women are not good for you. You had better learn and learn quickly to get past the exterior and find out about the interior. Beautiful women are a dime-a-dozen, seriously. God made them beautiful and voluptuous. But what you want, son, and what you had better get in a woman is a woman of virtue, integrity, trustworthiness and honor, if you want to have peace of mind in this life. Because if you fool around and get yourself a woman who is beautiful on the outside, yet on the inside she is full of lies, cheating, rebellion, stubbornness, disrespect, manipulation, etc., etc., you will have hell to pay! Mark my words.

Notice what Solomon says on this subject from the Book of Proverbs in the Holy Bible:

"Favour is deceitful, and beauty is vain: but a woman that feareth the Lord, she shall be praised."
—Proverbs 31: 30

"Who can find a virtuous woman? For her price is far above rubies."
—Proverbs 31:10

4. **As you are in the process of looking for that special someone, please put God first and the search for the right lady second**. Jesus said, *"But seek ye first the kingdom of God, and his righteousness; and all these things shall be added unto you."* (Matthew 6:33).

5. **Don't be afraid of women nor be intimidated by women**. They are just women. Love them, talk to them, lead them, have fun with them, but don't be afraid of them and don't be intimidated by them, because as soon as a woman detects that you are afraid of her or intimidated by her, you are doomed.

6. **I want to say to you also something that may be a shock to you, and that is: YOU ARE THE PRIZE TOO**. Yes, to find a good woman is a prize indeed, but contrary to what one might think, it is also a prize for a woman to find a good man in this day and time. And considering the male/female ratio in the black community, a woman finding a good man is more of a prize. So don't sell yourself short.

7. Another secret item that will help you understand the women folk **is the simple, untold, truth that women desire men just as much as men desire women** I am not only talking about in emotional, financial and romantic ways, but physically as well. This is just a normal thing that our Creator put in both the male and the female. So do not buy the myth that you have to bow to women and beg her to get interested in you. She may already be interested.

8. Take note with me the kind of men most women really like. And for some strange reason, it is not the soft, apologizing, shuffling, sweet, little, sugary man she is looking for. **Good women like real men**. Notice some things women like in men:

A. Confident, but not arrogant.
B. Cool, not hot-headed.
C. One who knows where he is going.
D. One who does not let women control and manipulate him. Women don't like weak-back men.
E. A clean and neat dresser.
F. One who can share his true feelings well.
G. One who is authentic.
H. A man who "knows" how to handle her.
I. A man who can make her laugh.
J. A man who will not let her have her way all of the time.
K. A man who likes to have sex often and who enjoys sex.

9. Here is something to keep in mind, that is not popular with men or women today: **In your relationship with the woman in your life, be the leade**r: "Be the head and not the tail." Don't be the follower. Understand, son, that God made you to be the leader of the relationship. This does not mean, in any way, that you have the right to be abusive or to mistreat her, however.

Lovingly insist that your relationship be this way because God intended for it to be this way. If you are a strong, loving leader, a "good woman" will not mind, at all, lining up with your leadership. Deep down in their heart of hearts, good, decent women appreciate strong, loving, decisive male leadership, and they despise or will eventually despise a man who is not a strong leader and who lets her control him and manipulate him. In fact, I know of countless cases where women left easy, soft, weak, "nicey, nicey" men who let them have their way, for strong, decisive men who did not let them have their way all of the time. It is a strange situation, but what I am telling you is true. Be a strong, loving man who knows where he is going, knows what he wants, who can think independently, and who does not allow women to hinder him. Strangely, women will be greatly attracted to you if you **genuinely** exude that kind of personality.

10. Contrary to what is popular today, pray for a good woman and marry young. This waiting until you are thirty and thirty-five years old is not wise. Get yourself a young, beautiful girl and marry her while you are young. This will save you a host of temptations and problems, and one of the great side benefits is that your children will be grown while you are still young. Brother man, if you don't have the gift of celibacy, which you probably don't have, please marry young. If you don't, you will probably end up doing things, sexually speaking, that you will regret the rest of your life. Do not think holding out for as long as you can is the best way.

I could write an entire book on this subject. But for now, just remember these things as you deal with the opposite sex.

Dealing With The Women Folk Well,

Daniel

P.T.:

■   *"God save us from wives who are angels in the street, saints in the church, and devils at home."*
                                                    —Spurgeon

■   *"Every wise woman buildeth her house: but the foolish plucketh it down with her hands."*
                                                    —Proverbs 14:1

■   *"It is better to dwell in the corner of the housetop,*

129

than with a brawling woman in a wide house."
—Proverbs 21:9

■ "It is better to dwell in the wilderness, than with a contentious and an angry woman."
—Proverbs 21: 19

■ "Favor is deceitful, and beauty is vain: but a woman that feareth the Lord, she shall be praised."
—Proverbs 31:30

■ "Such is the way of an adulterous woman; she eateth, and wipeth her mouth, and saith, I have done no wickedness."
—Proverbs 30:20

■ "Many receive advice, only the wise profit by it."
—Syrus

■ "If I take care of my character, my reputation will take care of itself."
—Unknown

THINK FOR YOURSELF!

Letter Twenty-four

Dear Y.B.M.:

One of the saddest things that I see today is so many people who do not think for themselves, especially young black men. It is painful to watch so many gullible people be led astray.

Think for yourself!

Be a leader instead of a follower. We have enough followers. These people let others think for them, speak for them and even do for them. Don't allow yourself to get into that rut. Think for yourself. Be the leader that God wants you to be.

Simply because a person is older and in a position of authority and is considered a leader by many, does not mean he has to be your leader. His perceived high position by many does not mean his ideas, statements and direction are correct. Think for yourself!

Now, in order to learn how to think for yourself, you need to do at least three things:

1. **You need to size up every "leader" and his statements with the rule book: the Bible**. You must see if what the person is saying is jiving with God's eternal Word.

2. **You need to have a set of convictions about the issues of life based upon a biblical foundation.** This way you are not swayed by every new wind of ideas that blow your way.

3. You need to examine what people say before you accept it "hook, line and sinker," so to speak.

In order to keep from going down the wrong path, in order to protect your family, in order to be the leader that God wants you to be, you must think for yourself and take responsibility for your statements, decisions and actions.

My friend, trust me: it is much easier to be a follower than it is to be a leader. But it is much better to think for yourself and be the leader that God wants you to be — the leader who is going right and who is leading others right.

Thinking For Myself,

Bro. Daniel

P.T.:

■ "It takes no courage to get in the back of a crowd and throw a rock."

—Thurgood Marshall

■ "It's never the right time to take a particular stand."

—Adam Clayton Powell, Jr.

■ "The ultimate measure of a man is not where he stands in moments of comfort and convenience, but where he stands at times of challenge and controversy."

—Dr. Martin Luther King, Jr.

■ "The hallmark of courage in this age of conformity is to stand up for what you believe."

—Courtland Milloy

■ "Fear is an illusion."

—Michael Jordan

SIGNING OFF FOR NOW

Letter Twenty-five

Dear Y.B.M.:

I trust that you are doing well today.

I pray and hope that you have enjoyed reading these letters just as much as I have enjoyed writing them to you. More importantly, though, I hope that you will apply these principles to your life, so that your life can be a grand success, and so that at the same time you can help others be a success as well.

As I sign off for a little while, allow me to leave you with a word from the wisest man who ever lived, King Solomon:

> *"Remember now thy Creator in the days of thy youth."*
> —Ecclesiastes 12:1

With Solomon, let me encourage you to remember the Lord in all that you do. Follow Him and serve Him throughout your life, and He will make you prosper and you will have good success. It will not be easy, but God will see you through.

Next time you hear from me, I will be writing to you in the book, *MO' Letters to Young Black Men: More Advice & Encouragement for A Difficult Journey.* Here are some of the subjects that I will deal with:

- Oh! The Mistakes I've Made
- Oh! The Troubles I've Seen
- How To Win Over Racism

- The Good White People
- Black on Black Racism
- How To Prosper Through Giving
- More 411 on Women Folk!
- Things You Must Do Today For Tomorrow
- When This Life Is Over

Well, until then: Pray! Think! Do!

Peace and a Long Life,

Daniel

DISCLAIMER ON QUOTATIONS

Simply because we included a certain quotation in this book, does not necessarily mean that we condone the lifestyle or belief system of the person quoted. We included quotations in this book totally based upon the actual meaning of the words of the quotation and its connection to a particular chapter and not upon the person who said it or wrote it.

HOW TO OBTAIN MORE COPIES OF
LETTERS TO YOUNG BLACK MEN

Our prayer and desire is to see a copy of this book in the hands of every young black man in America and around the world. You can assist in this great mission.

You can obtain more copies of this book in fine bookstores and other retail outlets across the United States of America.

OR

You may order extra copies via one of the websites listed below:

1. **www.torchlegacy.com**
2. **www.amazon.com**
3. **www.barnesandnoble.com**
4. **www.bamm.com** (Books-A-Million)
5. **www.borders.com**
6. **www.cbd.com** (Christian Book Distributors)

Contact Info:

Also, if you have any questions, comments, or need further encouragement, please feel free to e-mail me at:

DW3@torchlegacy.com

If you want to know more about getting to know your Creator, call:

1-877-TORCHLP

Look For...
MO' LETTERS TO YOUNG BLACK MEN

In fine bookstores and retail outlets across the United States and on the following websites:

1. www.torchlegacy.com
2. www.amazon.com
3. www.barnesandnoble.com
4. www.bamm.com (Books-A-Million)
5. www.borders.com
6. www.cbd.com (Christian Book Distributors)

• TO BE RELEASED IN 2006 •

In this sequel to *Letters To Young Black Men: Advice and Encouragement for a Difficult Journey*, Daniel Whyte III addresses more issues facing young black men in today's world. If you thought the first one was good, wait till you read *Mo' Letters To Young Black Men*.

Also, Look For...
EVEN MO' LETTERS TO YOUNG BLACK MEN
TO BE RELEASED IN 2007

This third volume will include letters from leading black men from various fields, as well as principles on leadership.

DANIEL'S TOP TEN COLLEGE PICKS FOR YOUNG BLACK MEN

(These colleges are not listed in any certain order.)

1. **Morehouse College**   Atlanta, GA
   800-851-1254

2. **Tuskegee University**   Tuskegee, AL
   800-622-6531

3. **Hampton University**   Hampton, VA
   800-624-3328

4. **Jarvis Christian College**   Hawkins, TX
   903-769-5700

5. **Howard University**   Washington, D.C.
   202-806-2763

6. **Fisk University**   Nashville, TN
   800-433-FISK

7. **Columbia University**   New York, NY
   212-854-2522

8. **Texas Wesleyan University**   Fort Worth, TX
   800-580-8980

9. **North Carolina A & T**   Greensboro, NC
   800-443-8964

10. **Florida A & M University**   Tallahassee, FL
    850-599-3000

Must Read Books For Young Black Men
(These Books Are Not Listed In Any Certain Order)

1. *No More Excuses: Be The Man God Made You To Be*
   by Dr. Tony Evans

2. *A Man's Role In The Home*
   by Dr. Tony Evans

3. *So You Call Yourself A Man?*
   by Bishop T. D. Jakes

4. *He-Motions*
   by Bishop T.D. Jakes

5. *How To Develop The Leader Within You*
   by John Maxwell

6. *Life is Tremendous*
   by Charles "Tremendous" Jones

7. *Do It Now!*
   by Ed Bliss

8. *The Seven Habits Of Highly Effective People*
   by Stephen Covey

9. *It Only Takes Everything You've Got*
   by Julio Melara

10. *The Power of Focus*
    by Jack Canfield, Mark Victor Hansen and Les Hewitt

11. *The Success Journey*
    by John Maxwell

50. ***When Black Preachers Preach Volumes I, II & III***
   Compiled and Edited by Daniel Whyte III

51. ***God Has Smiled On Me: A Tribute To A Black Father Who Stayed***
   by Daniel Whyte III

52. ***The Purpose Driven Life***
   by Rick Warren

Dear Y.B.M.:

Obviously, there are many other books that I would like to share with you, but my space is limited here. If you are interested in more information on other great books, please e-mail me at:

DW3@torchlegacy.com

Great Websites That Could Be of Help To You As A Young Black Man

(These Websites are not listed in any certain order)

1. www.blackhistory.com

2. www.focusonthefamily.org

3. www.100blackmen.org

4. www.cbmnational.org

5. www.tonyevans.org

6. www.blackandchristian.com

7. www.blackgospel.com

8. www.injoy.com

9. www.blackenterprise.com

10. www.hbcuconnect.com

11. www.gospelcity.com

12. www.black-collegian.com

13. www.tdjakes.org

14. www.sybm.org

15. www.torchlegacy.com

16. www.purposedrivenlife.com